RIGORS OF THE CALL

Also by
Beverly ND Clopton

SonShine: Reflections of Faith
Surviving Pitfalls on the Path
Heaven or Bust: Journey to Glory

Rigors of the Call

BEVERLY ND CLOPTON

WordCrafts

Rigors of the Call
Copyright © 2020
Beverly ND Clopton

Cover concept and design by Jonathan Grisham for Grisham Designs.

ISBN: 978-1-952474-04-0

All rights reserved. No part of this book may be reproduced, stored in a retrieval system, or transmitted in any form or by any means—electronic, mechanical, photocopy, recording or otherwise—without the prior written permission of the publisher. The only exception is brief quotations for review purposes.

All Scripture quotations are taken from THE HOLY BIBLE, NEW INTERNATIONAL VERSION®, NIV® Copyright © 1973, 1978, 1984, 2011 by Biblica, Inc.™ Used by permission. All rights reserved worldwide.

Published by WordCrafts Press
Cody, Wyoming 82414
www.wordcrafts.net

Contents

Introduction 1

Part I God's Call to the Ancients

Noah's Rigor 6
Abram/Abraham's Rigor 9
Moses' Rigor 13
David's Rigor 18
Daniel's Rigor 23
Jeremiah's Rigor 27
Hosea's Rigor 33
Finale 36

Part II God's Call to Jesus

Jesus' Rigor 44

Part III Jesus' Call to the Disciples

The Disciples' Rigor 50

Part IV Jesus' Call to the Apostle Paul

Apostle Paul's Rigor 57
Finale 62

Part V God's Call to 21st Century Christians

The Rigor of 21st Century Christian Identity 65
The Rigor of 21st Century Christian Obedience 69
The Rigor of 21st Century Christian Labor 73

Part VI Final Thoughts

Acknowledgements 84
About the Author 86

Introduction

The minister's sermon title was "*What Everyone Should Know About Pastoring.*" He began his message with the comment that being a pastor is difficult. As he swept his pointed finger across the expanse of the pews, he said the reason it's difficult is because those whom pastors are called to pastor are themselves difficult. The statement predictably was met with laughter from the congregation. He continued by offering examples of the many challenges pastors face as they respond to God's call to follow Him and in so doing to shepherd His people.

As I listened to his sermon the idea sprang to mind that what the pastor detailed as difficult and hard in following God's call was applicable not only to pastors, but to all believers; that the call to follow Jesus (to follow God) is not a leisurely walk along silvery white beaches where crystal blue waves softly wash ashore. Rather, more often than not, the call sends believers dashing for cover as storm clouds filled with the antithesis of their faith loom threateningly above.

According to the Pew Research Center, 2.2 billion people

around the world identify themselves as Christians. Those who today claim this faith live in an era not unlike those of their biblical ancestors; a time when *godlessness is on the throne and godliness on the scaffold*. This book is written for and about these 2.2 billion Christ/God followers, and perhaps for those contemplating becoming one of them. I write it more convinced than ever that the invitation to follow Jesus/God is easier to accept than it is to execute. As we mature in faith, we soon enough confront the rigor inherent in the call to faith. Saying "Yes" to God/to Jesus is hard.

An online dictionary lists more than 12 definitions or synonyms for the term "rigor" under the subheading of "demanding, difficult, or extreme conditions." The chapters that follow will speak to those conditions.

Rigor is hard. In Pete Souza's photo book, *Obama, An Intimate Portrait,* about the presidency of Barack Obama, I noticed in one picture a plaque that read *"Hard things are hard."* That simplistic statement speaks truth to the difficulties God's people, both clergy and laity, experience as they weather hardships, suffering, adversity, distress, and trying times intrinsic in God's call. Our Lord knew that sooner than later the reality of the rigor would face all who heard the call to go, to do, to be, to follow. Jesus' words to those New Testament first responders ring true:

> *"In this world you will have trouble. But take heart! I have overcome the world."*
> John 16:33

Beginning with scriptural accounts that highlight some of our biblical ancestors and ending with contemporary

Christians and their faith experiences, this book will explore the rigor, both then and now, of being a believer in God and His Son Jesus, and how the rigor of responding to their call helps to shape us for eternity.

The book is divided into four parts. Part One traces God's call to some of the ancients who heard and heeded His summons and in so doing confronted the rigor of that call. Part Two examines a topic not often explored: God's call to His son Jesus and the rigor He faced in response. Parts Three and Four move through the New Testament and Jesus' call to the 12 disciples and to the apostle Paul to show how the rigor of the call tested their faith. Part Five looks at Christians of the modern era for whom the call remains the same and the rigor of embracing or adhering to it as difficult because *"Hard things are hard."*

Part I

God's Call to the Ancients

So, God created mankind in his own image, in the image of God he created them; male and female he created them.
Genesis 1:27

Christians generally accept that God created humankind to be more than just custodians of His nonhuman creatures and the earth itself. Those who claim the faith understand that He primarily created us to be in fellowship with Him and to worship Him alone as the one and only God. Initially our nascent biblical ancestors got that. They enjoyed the garden home in which they resided, the nourishment provided therein, and the times of fellowship with God when He strolled "in the garden in the cool of the day."

The third chapter of the book of Genesis details the reasons the relationship between the Creator and the man and woman fell apart, and they were banished forever from the garden. But because of His love for His human creation, God never gave up on them. Divine Plan B emerged and in due time was set in motion. He would repair the brokenness between Creator and humanity and bring them back into relationship with Him. He gave opportunities to selected individuals to respond to His call by following His commands; and if they were obedient, the brokenness caused by the disobedience in the garden would be repaired.

As these individuals would discover, God's call would not be easy or without difficulties. Oftentimes the effort to respond to His call would test their faith. These are their stories, sometimes reimagined, but their stories nonetheless. Each story offers hope that even when the task seems beyond our abilities, we can meet the rigor of the divine call if we cling in faith to the divine one who is calling.

1

NOAH'S RIGOR

Chapter six of the book of Genesis introduces us to Noah, *"a righteous man, blameless among the people of his time, and he walked faithfully with God."* (Genesis 6:9) Right away we know Noah is someone who has heard the call of God and responded to it—*"he walked faithfully with God."* At this juncture in biblical accounting, God is so fed up with mankind's continuing sin that He's ready to throw in the towel and start over.

> *"So, the Lord said, 'I will wipe from the face of the earth the human race I have created... for I regret that I have made them.'"*
>
> Genesis: 7-8

But Noah found favor in the eyes of the Lord. It stands to reason that if Noah is the only human living righteously among the multitude of corrupt humans, he is probably not the most popular guy in the neighborhood. In all likelihood, folks shot dismissive glances his way, crossed to the other side of the road to avoid speaking to him, kept their children from playing with his, and generally considered him a collective thorn in their sides. Thus, you know without scripture telling us specifically that when he started building an ark at God's command, the proverbial droppings hit the fan.

Thanks to cinematic interpretations of scripture, most of us accept the reactions of the people in Noah's community, though the Bible does not specifically provide this information. It's easy for us to embrace the traditions formed by storytellers, commentators, and movie producers, that portray the community showering Noah with ridicule every time he was engaged in his ark building. In our mind's eye, we can envision the scene as mocking and scornful words are hurled at him and his sons as they implement God's ark instructions.

As year after year passed with no sign of rain, we can imagine that those sarcastic and disparaging remarks grew harder to bear. And as the faithful Noah worked day after day, it's not far-fetched to say that even he may have wondered, *"Why me, Lord. Why me? How much longer must I bear this? When is this rain you spoke of coming? And come to think of it, how exactly are my three sons and I supposed to gather all these animals and herd them onto the ark? My neighbors think I'm looney, so they're certainly not going to help us."*

We also have no record of the three sons embracing this ark building project with enthusiasm. Even in a time when children obeyed their parents without question, it's not hard to believe there might have been some under the breath grumbling as time passed, weeks turning to months and months to years with the construction work dominating their lives. Biblical experts estimate the time frame for the ark's completion to have been between 40–50 years.

Let's hit the pause button right about now in Noah's story and ponder these very real reactions of a man who heard the divine call of God and committed to following Him. We understand that Noah's faithfulness did not exempt him from the rigor that faithfulness demands. Perhaps this is the first reality faced by those who hear God's call.

The second reality is that in none of the stories we explore does God ever present the call as something easy, without risks, inopportune, or without challenge. Rather when He calls, those who respond should expect rigor to be inherent in their execution of the call.

That rigor was required of Noah is an understatement. Despite constant verbal abuse uttered by the people of his community and no physical evidence of rain, to say nothing of epic flooding, Noah demonstrated one of the virtues that rigor demands: steadfastness when what God calls you to do flies in the face of common sense and reason. The lines of Rudyard Kipling's iconic poem "If" speak to this moment in Noah's life: "If you can trust yourself when all men doubt you…"

Noah didn't just trust himself, he trusted God. That proved enough. For what might have seemed impossible through human eyes was possible from God's perspective. During all the years of enduring the rigor of ridicule, Noah's faith did not diminish. His obedience and faithfulness to what God called him to do secured his place in eternity.

2

Abram/Abraham's Rigor

> *"The Lord had said to Abram, 'Leave your country, your people and your father's household and go to the land I will show you. I will make you into a great nation and I will bless you; I will make your name great,' ... So, Abram left, as the Lord had told him; ... Abram was seventy-five years of age when he set out from Haran."*
>
> Genesis 12:1-4

Unlike Noah's, God's call to Abram has not lent itself to reimagining on the big screen and thus becoming part of the collective secular culture. Still, he was destined for renown, becoming the first of the Jewish patriarchs revered by the three largest monotheistic religions—Judaism, Christianity, and Islam. At the time of his call, he was a 75-year-old married man still living in his daddy's house. Prior to this proclamation from the Lord, scripture reveals little about Abram that might explain why God selected to bestow all these promises upon an AARP-eligible man. What we perceive about him comes after God's call. *"So, Abram left, as the Lord had told him...."* That action and his belief earned him God's affirmation, *"Abram believed the Lord, and he credited it to him as righteousness,"* seemingly set him apart.

Age obviously is of little concern to God. At what to us seems a rather late-in-life summons to embark upon such a journey speaks to God's concept of time; and that His plans depend not on one's age, but one's willingness to say "yes" to His call. It goes without saying that age and status were inconsequential to obedience, belief, and faith, those being the distinguishing traits Abram demonstrated by his actions to go with his wife and nephew to the land to which God would lead him.

It doesn't take a graduate degree in theology to grasp the rigor God's call required of our obedient and faith-filled septuagenarian. Surely the journey itself tested his physical stamina, and as his story unfolded, his integrity (though he failed this test when he instructed Sarai to pretend to be his sister, so the Egyptians won't kill him—Genesis 12:10-20), his loyalty to family, and eventually his belief in God to deliver on His promise. If we understand rigor to be what we've identified: difficult, demanding, strenuous, exasperating, it's easy to point to all of these markers in the patriarch's life.

As his journey continued, and before God changed his name from Abram to Abraham, he faced the rigor of making a decision destined to leave its imprint upon humankind forever. His wife decided she had waited long enough for a child and told Abram to sleep with her maidservant in hopes a pregnancy would result. She reasoned it would be a way for them to build a family. Because he knew what God had told him regarding his future descendants, it must have been an agonizing decision to make—wait for God to deliver or agree to his wife's demand. Scripture reads, *"Abram agreed to what Sarai said."*

We can probably trace our daytime soap operas to the drama in the tent after Haggar conceived and bore a son. Once again, what God intended for His people fell prey to their decisions to create their own destiny. Yet, He did not give up on the patriarch. In due time, at an even more advanced age, God fulfilled His promise to Abraham, and Sarah bore a son they named Isaac. God was faithful to His promise. Yet even as that promise manifested in the birth of his son, the rigor of his calling would confront Abraham in a way he could have never imagined.

> *"Then God said, 'Take your son, your only son, Isaac, whom you love, and go to the region of Moriah. Sacrifice him there as a burnt offering on one of the mountains I will tell you about.'"*

Genesis: 22:2

We can only surmise that by the time Abraham hears these words of God, he is well settled into the adventures of domestic life. His beloved son is at least 12, and knowledgeable of the rituals of sacrifice as his question to his father when they reach the sacrifice site suggests, *"'...but where is the lamb for the burnt offering?'"*

We can also surmise that this time God's call was a lot more difficult than the initial one to which Abraham responded. Though God had pronounced early on that Abraham's faith accorded him the label of "righteousness," this is dramatically different. This is that moment in contemporary speak when the "rubber hits the road." It's a "ride or die" time of the test of one's loyalty. We need not stretch our imaginations to sense Abraham's internal struggle as he wrestles with the reasonableness of God's call juxtaposed with His promises regarding Isaac, and the command to sacrifice him. How can the promise of the former be realized in the obedience to the latter?

We marvel at Abraham's ability to make preparations for this heartbreaking task; to obey God in a situation that defies reason; with certainty that God will deliver on the promise He makes though the situation suggests otherwise. Without doubt this is primetime "rigor of the call;" a time when faith is challenged by reason and a promise negated by a contrary command. Yet the patriarch continues in obedience and is stopped from slaughtering his only son only when the Lord intervenes. (Genesis 22:8-12)

At his advanced age, Abraham surely thought he was done with the rigors that responding "Yes" to God's call can bring. His story reminds us otherwise. As long as we strive to be faithful to God, He will call. The design of those calls will differ for each of us, and whatever form they take, we should expect rigor to be a given.

3

Moses' Rigor

> *So Moses thought, "I will go over and see this strange sight–why the bush does not burn up." When the Lord saw that he had gone over to look, God called to him from within the bush, "Moses! Moses! And Moses said, "Here I am." ... The Lord said, "I have indeed seen the misery of my people in Egypt ... and I have seen the way the Egyptians are oppressing them. So now, go. I am sending you to Pharaoh to bring my people the Israelites out of Egypt."*
>
> Exodus 3:3-10

Even before he began the work God was calling him to do, Moses was hit with the rigor of that call. What God wanted was exasperating because it forced him to deal with his insecurities, his fears, and even perhaps his guilt. During four decades of tending sheep, those emotions had been deeply buried. Then, without warning, came God's call.

Whether one is Christian or not, the epic story of Moses leading the exodus from Egypt and his parting of the Red

Sea is as well known in our popular culture as that of Noah and the great flood. Multiple dramatic interpretations of it have played in movie theaters and on television screens for decades. However, unlike Noah, who seemingly heard God's call and without hesitation responded to it, Moses was a little more like many of us might have been—he gave excuses as to why he couldn't possibly do what God was asking him to do.

"Who am I, that I should go to Pharaoh and bring the Israelites out of Egypt?" (Sorry, God, but that's just not my skill-set, and just as importantly, it's above my pay grade.) *"Suppose I go to the Israelites and say to them, 'The God of your fathers has sent me to you,' and they ask me, 'What is his name?' Then what shall I say?"* (God, these people don't really know me; and what am I supposed to say to convince them that it's really God who sent me? No way, this will work.) *"What if they do not believe me or listen to me, and say, 'The Lord did not appear to you'?"* (Let's be real, God. These people will think I'm a nut case if I approach them like I'm responding to something You have literally told me to do.) Yes, Moses began his storied walk with the Lord with great reluctance and insecurities.

Maybe he had divided loyalties—a Hebrew himself who would have been among the oppressed he was being sent to rescue, but who had been spared by being adopted by the Pharaoh's daughter and raised in the Pharaoh's royal court. Perhaps the fear of facing the consequences for the crime he had committed while still a member of the royal family gave him pause. The Bible does not illuminate the underlying reasons Moses initially resisted God's call. What it does tell is that God's anger burned against Moses when seemingly in desperation, he finally protested, *"O Lord, please send someone else to do it."* (Exodus 3:13)

Despite His anger at Moses' resistance to His call, God didn't throw up His hands and move on. He implemented Plan B; Moses' brother Aaron was appointed to accompany Moses and help him deliver God's messages to the king. Both the Bible and the big screen capture our attention as Moses and Aaron deliver God's command to free the Israelites; the Pharaoh refuses and God responds by sending a variety of plagues. Only when the last plague kills the first born of the Egyptians does Pharaoh relent and free God's people. We hold our breath as they march out of Egypt and all too soon are blocked by a sea looming in front of them and the army of Pharaoh behind in hot pursuit. We marvel as Moses raises his staff, the sea waters part, and the people begin the miraculous crossing on dry land while a pillar of fire stations itself between the Egyptian army and the Israelites until they are safely on the other side. As they look backwards, the sea waters flow back into place, drowning the entire army that had attempted to follow them.

Though our Bible doesn't speak to it, we imagine at this moment of victory, any lingering doubts Moses might have had about being cast in the role of liberator are distant thoughts as the people burst forth in songs of praise and thanksgiving to God and Moses. Perhaps hoisted upon the shoulders of Aaron and Joshua, Moses raises the staff toward heaven and joins in the singing. The initial exasperation he felt when God tapped him to go to Egypt no longer haunts him. God was right; he could lead these people, his people, to the promised land. Little does he realize that the rigor of God's call is not finished. It in fact has just begun.

A short three days into the journey, the people begin their initial grumbling and complaining. The available water is bitter. Following God's instructions, Moses solves that issue. Then *"on the fifteenth day of the second month after they had come out of Egypt,"* the grumbling starts again. This time it's the food or lack thereof.

> *"If only we had died by the Lord's hand in Egypt. There we sat around pots of meat and ate all the food we wanted…"*
> Exodus 16:3

From this point onward, Moses will grapple with words not yet penned: *"these are the times that try men's souls."* (Thomas Paine) And as the days become weeks, the weeks become months, and the months turn into years, this freedom fighter will know not only how exasperating God's call is, but how demanding obedience to it can be.

Through the next three books of the Old Testament (Leviticus, Numbers, and Deuteronomy), Moses attempts to lead God's people to the land He had promised their ancestors. It's a constant struggle as the people obey God's commandments for a while and then with short memories of their past revert to sinful behaviors that violate them.

One of their most egregious transgressions is worthy of note. If ever Moses regretted responding to the Lord's call, it most certainly might have been when the people in stark disobedience decide his absence is reason to find another God to worship; even though they knew God's first commandment was,

> *"I am the Lord your God, who brought you out of Egypt, out of the land of slavery. You shall have no other gods before me."*
> Exodus 20:2-3

They convinced Aaron to build a golden calf that they could worship, declaring,

> *"Come, make us gods who will go before us. As for this fellow Moses who brought us up out of Egypt, we don't know what has happened to him."*
> Exodus 32:1

When Moses returned to the camp and saw the calf fashioned from gold and the people singing and dancing around it, he was beyond exasperation. The people were running wild about the camp and in his anger at what they had done, Moses threw the stone tablets upon which were written the Ten Commandments to the ground, breaking them to pieces, an understandable demonstration of his vexation and anger at what these "stiff necked" people had done.

The people whom he had been called to lead would continue in their vacillating relationship with God for many years. As Moses recounts their dubious commitment in chapters nine and ten of the book of Deuteronomy, we understand his intense aggravation and grasp how difficult attempting to lead them must have been. From a hesitant shepherd called by God from a burning bush to a faithful liberator and defender of a decidedly double-minded people, Moses—the man who the Bible proclaims knew the Lord "face to face"—stands among the ancient prophets of our faith who knew firsthand the rigor inherent in the answering of God's call.

4

David's Rigor

"Then the Lord said, 'Rise, and anoint him; he is the one.'"
1 Samuel 16:12

And with these words spoken by God to His prophet Samuel, David, the youngest son of Jesse of Bethlehem, is called by God to be king. On that day, *"the Spirit of the Lord came upon David in power."* (1 Samuel 16:13) Though the young man did not know it at the time, the rigor ingrained in God's call had been set in motion before this moment. As he had cared for his father's sheep, his reactions to the threats of wild animals seemed to foreshadow his destiny.

God knew David's heart as the apostle Paul so writes,

"I have found David, son of Jesse a man after my own heart; he will do everything I want him to do."
Acts 13:22

David's saga, like those of the other ancient witnesses to

God's power, required of him a spirit of faithfulness, obedience, and courage. It would be in his efforts to do what God called him to do that he would face the rigor therein.

We know David did not proceed immediately to the throne. In fact, after he was filled with God's spirit, he first went back to the fields and there continued to guard his father's sheep. Sometime later (scripture is not clear on how much time elapsed), David is summoned to King Saul's palace to play his harp. It seemed the king was slipping more and more into a state of mental madness, and the servants persuaded him to have a young shepherd attend him as a remedy for his mental illness. As time passed, David shuttled between the fields and the palace: shepherding sheep and playing the harp for a mad king.

One day he is sent by his father with food for his older brothers, members of Saul's army engaged in battle with the Philistines. David soon finds himself the only Israelite brave enough to fight Goliath, the enemy's giant hero. His killing of Goliath with a slingshot and a single stone is legendary. Afterwards as he and the soldiers returned home, the people sang,

> *"Saul has slain his thousands, and David his tens of thousands."*
> 1 Samuel 18:7

King Saul's reaction—anger and jealousy.

Throughout the remaining chapters of 1 Samuel, David realized that his anointing to the kingship is not going to be an easy one to claim. King Saul's increasing rage and mental instability force David into hiding, in fear of his life. That's what you do when one day as you sit playing your harp, the king for whom you are playing suddenly throws a spear at you in an attempt to pin you to the wall behind.

Neither biblical scholars nor the Bible itself gives certainty to how much time elapses between Saul's first attempt to kill David and David's ascension to the throne. What we do know is that during the time of hiding in fields and evading Saul by residing in the land of the Philistines, David's realization of God's call to be king is wrought with difficulty. Even the times that on the surface presented themselves as opportunities for victory became testing times for David; and testing times are always hard. They sometimes require of the tested qualities that go against the norms.

On two such occasions, David had the chance to kill Saul, but he chose not to. Once as depicted in 1 Samuel, chapter 24, David and his men were hiding in a cave when Saul came into it to relieve himself. Imagine the temptation to do what his men were urging, quoting to him God's words, *"I will give your enemy into your hands to do with as you wish."* Yet, more than claiming victory, David chose to honor Saul because he was God's anointed. Again, when David came upon Saul asleep with his men as recorded in chapter 26 of 1 Samuel, he refused to allow his men to kill the king; opting only to take his sword as evidence that it had been within his power to do so if he wished. The restraint required to stop short of killing the man who sought to kill him was without doubt hard to pass up. Yet David did just that, saying, *"But the Lord forbid that I should lay a hand on the Lord's anointed."*

As scripture details in the 2 Samuel, following Saul's death David is finally anointed and proclaimed king. During his 40-year reign we witness him face the rigor of God's call to be king with fortitude, determination, and faith. He conquered Jerusalem, recaptured the ark, defeated the Philistines, and brought many other nations under his dominion. Yet even as his victories mounted, his story took an unexpected turn that seemed to negate his moniker: "a man after God's own heart."

The Bible reads,

> *"In the spring, at the time when kings go off to war, David sent Joab out with the king's men and the whole Israelite army. They destroyed the Ammonites and besieged Rabbah. But David remained in Jerusalem."*
> 2 Samuel 11:1

Why King David chose to stay at home during the traditional time when kings went to war is unknown. Scripture doesn't give insight into his motives. With nothing written that helps us understand what might have prompted him to sit this one out, we draw our conclusions based upon his actions. Thus, it is easy to term his decision to forfeit leadership of his army to his general a dereliction of his duty. At a time when responding to the rigor of God's call at the battlefront was what he should have been doing, King David instead was strolling the rooftop of his palace. His position placed him not on a bloody battlefield of men with lashing swords, but on a tempting bed of lust. Forgetting who God had anointed him to be, David yielded to the desires of his flesh.

Across the courtyard he spied a woman who was bathing; and though discovering she was married to one of his officers, he nonetheless committed adultery with her. As described in the 11th and 12th chapters of 1 Samuel, his decision had tragic and far reaching consequences.

David's story is stamped with dual portraits of living in relationship with God. How does a man whom God chose to be king because he was "a man after God's own heart" exemplify both rising to the demands of the rigor of God's call on the one hand and failing it on the other? Maybe the answer is simply that David forgot that one of rigor's core demands is self-denial. God's call demands sacrifice, and sacrifice means denying oneself of something that has the potential to impede one's answering of the call.

David, this man who because of God's call denied himself the satisfaction of killing the man who sought his life, was unable to shun the temptation of another man's wife. Perhaps David's story highlights yet another aspect of the rigor of the call. That aspect is the understanding that the rigor of God's call requires owning one's transgressions, seeking forgiveness, and then living with the consequences of our sin without abandoning God's call.

5

DANIEL'S RIGOR

Daniel was neither God's prophet nor king. At first glance he does not seem comparable to the biblical ancients mentioned in the earlier chapters. God did not call him to "go" as He did Abram and Moses; He did not call him to "do" as He did Noah. But as we unfold his story, we discover he was a man who throughout his life never wavered from adherence to his faith. God's call to Daniel was to stand firmly in his religious traditions and be faithful to the God he worshipped; and in so doing experience the rigor of the call.

Following Jerusalem's fall to King Nebuchadnezzar of Babylonia, the king ordered the chief of his court officials

> *"to bring from the royal family and the nobility–young men…showing aptitude for every kind of learning, well informed, quick to understand, and qualified to serve in the king's palace."*
>
> Daniel 1:3-4

Daniel and three other young men from Judah were among

those selected. As scripture records, the chief court official gave them new Babylonian names, a practice intended to erase the identity of the captured and make them more subservient to their new culture. This assault upon his religious heritage was but the first of the rigors Daniel would experience during his time of exile. He might be called by a pagan name, but he knew who he was and the God whom he served.

Immediately he distinguished himself as a man committed to his faith and the active living of it; a difficult thing to do in a pagan world.

> *"But Daniel resolved not to defile himself with the royal food and wine, and he asked the chief official for permission not to defile himself this way."*
> Daniel 1:8

The young men of Judah were captives, far from home and the sanctuary of a faith community that offered support. How easy it would have been to accept the practices of their pagan captors—to go along to get along. Why make life any more difficult than it was already? The answer is simple. Daniel's faith was non-negotiable. He accepted the difficulty of maintaining that faith in a foreign land; he did not shrink from the rigor such a posture demanded.

Daniel's reputation as a wise man and interpreter of dreams grew. There is no scripture which suggests that during those years, he fell away from his faith convictions. Rather he endured his captivity while maintaining the Levitical laws. When King Darius (Though Darius is mentioned in the Bible, no secular history of him exists. Biblical scholars suggest it may instead have been Cyrus the Great) decided to set to him over the whole kingdom, the other

> "administrators and the satraps tried to find grounds for charges against Daniel in his conduct of government affairs, but they were unable to do so.... Finally, these men said, 'We will never find any basis for charges against this man Daniel unless it has something to do with the law of his God."
>
> Daniel 6:1-5

In a plot worthy of any of today's books or movies, the administrators and satraps (governors) convinced the king to issue an edict that required everyone to pray 30 days only to the king. Violators of the edict were to be thrown into a den of lions as punishment. The "executive order" was signed and published.

Biblical scholarship suggests that Daniel was a teenager of perhaps 15 when he was led away to Babylonia around 606 BC. The Bible records that the Israelite captivity lasted 70 years. At the time of this royal decree, Daniel would have been a senior citizen well into his eighth decade. The words of scripture noted above give credence to the conclusion that he had managed to balance the secular demands of captivity with the sacred demands of his faith for a long time. We might understand if he had grown weary of the balancing act. If now as an octogenarian he had decided to fudge, to pray to the king and to his God—to the former in public and to the latter in secret—it would surely have been less of a burden. But as did the others who had risen to the demands of the rigor of God's calling, Daniel threw down the gauntlet.

> *"Now when Daniel learned that the decree had been published, he went home to his upstairs room where the windows opened toward Jerusalem. Three times a day he got down on his knees and prayed, giving thanks to his God, just as he had done before."*
>
> Daniel 6:10

The scene of Daniel on his knees praying to his God fades into that of the officials gleefully bringing this news to the king, demanding that Daniel be held accountable for disobeying the king's edict. The story of Daniel in the lions' den is widely known. It is told with an underlying message of God's protection in the midst of trial and tribulation. It is an acknowledged "miracle story." But as importantly, Daniel's experience in a lions' den testifies to the rigor of the call.

Weighing the consequences of his choices, Daniel showed no hesitation in choosing to obey God. More than likely it wasn't easy, but he accepted the difficulty that living his faith convictions required. Faithfulness to God at all costs was the rigor to which he was called.

6

Jeremiah's Rigor

Jeremiah was not the only prophet in service to God during the years that preceded the nation of Israel's 70-year exile to Babylonia. But only he among his contemporaries—the prophets Zephaniah, Habakkuk, and Ezekiel—came to be known as "the weeping prophet." That sobriquet distinguishes him and is often the only thing many believers know of his story.

Call his name and the image of a hoary, tearful biblical figure springs to mind. During the 40 years of his service as a prophetic voice to the surviving Jewish nation of Judah in what is now southern Israel (the northern Jewish nation having already been conquered by the Assyrians before Jeremiah's time), he would earn that nickname many times over. Indeed, it was in the earning of that moniker that Jeremiah would come to know the rigor of God's call to *do*, to *go*, and to *be*.

> *"The word of the Lord came to me, saying, 'Before I formed you in the womb, I knew you, before you were born, I set you*

apart; I appointed you as a prophet to the nations.'"
Jeremiah 1:4-5

Upon hearing these words, young Jeremiah protested to God that he had the wrong guy; he was not old enough; and did not know how to speak. Somewhat like his biblical ancestor, Moses, Jeremiah felt inadequate to serve as the Lord's spokesperson. But as God had countered Moses, He likewise rebuked Jeremiah's protestations, replying,

"Do not say, 'I am too young. You must go to everyone I send you to and say whatever I command you. Do not be afraid of them, for I am with you and will rescue you...'"
Jeremiah 1:7-8

With that declaration and the subsequent touching of Jeremiah's mouth as a sign that the words he spoke were God's words, Jeremiah was appointed...

"to uproot and tear down, to destroy and overthrow, to build and to plant."
Jeremiah 1:9-10

The little we know of the young man Jeremiah is limited to a brief bio sketch in the opening chapter of his book. He was the son of Hilkiah, a priest of Benjamite lineage. Perhaps what we may conclude is that as the son of a priest, he had grown up immersed in the faith of his ancestors and was a covenant believer in God; and though he was hesitant in accepting God's call, he did not appear startled by it. This suggests that he was probably an observant Jewish youth, unlike the stereotypical *preacher's kid* who is often bent upon rebellion against the restraints of his upbringing. Despite his initial resistance, God's words and touch were sufficient for him to embrace the Lord's call.

At the time Jeremiah began his ministry, the nation was in full blown rebellion. God's people were sinful, living in violation of every law God had given them. Not even the temple priests were in one accord with the God they purported to serve. Imagine this young adult stepping forward to confront and condemn the lifestyles and practices of not just his peers, but his elders and leaders, both sacred and secular; and saying to them—*"Hear what the Lord says to you, people of Israel. This is what the Lord says..."* Can we say *hard*? Can we proclaim *difficult*? Can we declare *rigorous*? Yes, we can, to all of these descriptors. What Jeremiah embraced in his God-led confrontations with his people was this and more. As might be said in contemporary lexiconic terms, it was "off the chain."

Over the next 20-plus years, Jeremiah would speak the word of God to an errant people. His prophecies were sharp and cut to the heart of the Lord's case against them. In a sort of thesis statement, God said,

> *"My people have committed two sins; they have forsaken me, the spring of living water, and have dug their own cisterns, broken cisterns that cannot hold water."*
> Jeremiah 2:13

In the succeeding chapters, Jeremiah offered proof in support of God's charges by specifically identifying the sins to which God referred:

- apostasy—the people abandoned their belief in the God who had delivered their forefathers and mothers and brought them out of slavery to His promised lands.
- idolatry—the people built their own gods, worshipped them and committed sacrilegious acts in God's house in their worship practices and the forbidden sacrifice of their children.
- adultery—the people were unfaithful, defied God's laws, and committed acts of sacred and secular infidelity.

Now 20-plus years of public exhortations, of preaching on the corner, standing perhaps on a wooden box, ignoring the boos and other unprintable expressions of disdain by folk walking by, was disheartening. As the years passed, Jeremiah knew this command of God's he sought to obey was more than daunting. It was tiring. It was hard. It was unending. These were sinful and hard-headed people. And as might be expected, in time they turned their disdain of God upon His messenger. The rigor Jeremiah had faced thus far would become even more challenging.

Jeremiah had probably grown accustomed to the mockery of his prophesying; but the first threat to his life was a game changer. The men of Anathoth said to him,

> *"Do not prophesy in the name of the Lord or you will die by our hands."*
>
> Jeremiah 11:21

This rejection of God's message by the men of his hometown is a harbinger of Jesus' experience in His hometown of Nazareth. As the Gospel of Luke records in chapter four,

Jesus' teachings in the synagogue outraged the people. Before they drove Him out of town and attempted to throw Him down a cliff, He proclaimed in their hearing, "*I tell you the truth, no prophet is accepted in his hometown.*"

Jeremiah's rigor did not end with these initial threats. As he steadfastly spoke the words God commanded him to speak, counter-claims and false prophesies were simultaneously uttered by false prophets. The continuous "Fake News" of the day most surely weighed heavily upon him. We grasp his anguish in chapter 20, verses 7-8, when he lifts his complaints to God of the ridicule, insults, and reproach he's enduring; and we feel his sorrow when he even laments that he had been born.

The difficulty of obeying God's call did not lessen. On the contrary, Jeremiah would receive more death threats (Jeremiah 26); he would be imprisoned (Jeremiah 20); verbal attacks would continue (Jeremiah 18); God would forbid him to marry—he was to remain celibate (Jeremiah 16); God would command him to wear a yoke upon his shoulders as a symbol of the yoke of submission the people would soon wear under the dominance of the Babylonian empire.

As the day of Jerusalem's fall drew nearer,

> "*this word came to Jeremiah from the Lord: 'Take a scroll and write upon it all the words I have spoken to you concerning Israel, Judah, and all the other nations from the time I began speaking to you in the reign of Josiah til now.*'"
> Jeremiah 36:1-2

As evidence of His unfailing love toward His people despite their continuing rejection of Him, God offered them an out. Perhaps if the verbal words of the prophet were written for them to hear, they would turn from their wickedness and receive God's forgiveness. (Jeremiah 36:3) Alas, not even this grand offer of redemption touched the heart of King Jehoiakim. Upon hearing the words of the scroll, he ordered it burned.

But the will of God is never thwarted. The scroll of Jeremiah's prophesies was rewritten and survives today in the book called by his name. Neither additional beatings nor arrests kept this prophet from the call of God. He would live beyond the destruction of Jerusalem that he prophesized; his last words recorded in chapter 51 of Jeremiah.

The tears of the *weeping prophet* give testament to a man who heard God's call and confronted the rigor therein with faithfulness, obedience, and courage.

7

HOSEA'S RIGOR

The rigor inherent in Hosea's call can be summarized in one word: onerous, an adjective the dictionary says is used when speaking of a task, duty, or responsibility that is difficult and oppressively burdensome. It is an apt description of what God's call came to be in the life of this minor prophet who served during the reigns of five kings.

Written to the northern kingdom of Israel before that nation was exiled to Assyria, the book of Hosea is divided into two distinct parts. Chapters 1-3 speak primarily of Hosea's personal life and its juxtaposition with God's personal relationship with His people. The remaining chapters are God's discourses relative to Israel's sins and prospective punishments if they do not return to their covenant relationship with Him. Throughout each, the rigor would haunt Hosea each time God spoke the words to be proclaimed to an unfaithful nation.

> *"When the Lord began to speak through Hosea, the Lord said to him, 'Go marry a promiscuous woman and have*

children with her, for like an adulterous wife this land is guilty of unfaithfulness to the Lord.' So he married Gomer daughter of Diblaim, and she bore him a son."
Hosea 1:2-3

With this child and the succeeding daughter and son Gomer bore, God drove the stake of rigor even deeper. He commanded Hosea to give the children names not in the traditional manner of choosing one that might express hopes for the child's future; but rather names that spoke to God's displeasure with the kingdom of Israel. Of the first born, He said to Hosea, *"Call him Jezreel, because I will soon punish the house of Jehu for the massacre at Jezreel, and I will put an end to the kingdom of Israel."* At the birth of the daughter, God said to Hosea, *"Call her Ruhamah,* (meaning *not loved) for I will no longer show love to the house of Israel, that I should at all forgive them."* And at the birth of the third child, God said, *"Call him Lo-Ammi,* (meaning *not my people) for you are not my people and I am not your God."* (Hosea 1:4-9)

Imagine the difficulty of obeying these divine pronouncements; by their names his children would forever be symbolic of God's anger and disillusionment toward his people. Yet in faithfulness, Hosea bore the burden of his calling and continued to do as God directed.

At some point, following the birth of the second son, Lo-Ammi, Gomer left Hosea and the children and resumed her former profession as a *working girl*. Scripture shines no light upon Hosea's emotional state at that turn of events. But judging by what we know of human nature, his wife's desertion had to have been hard. Though the marriage was not one he had sought, but one commanded of him by God,

Gomer's behavior was but a painful reminder of what he had been called by God to do. He had wed a known prostitute. Conceivably, at the beginning of the marriage he may not have had feelings for her, but as time passed that could have changed. After all, she was the mother of his children.

While there is no scriptural discourse regarding the emotional impact of her departure, again assumptions are possible. The embarrassment of an unfaithful wife; three motherless children; prophesies that fell upon deaf ears—these were circumstances that would put a slump in the shoulders of the mightiest of men. If Hosea was anything like us, at this point he was probably thinking, "*I have been obedient and done what God told me to do. Gomer's gone; I'll get over what she did; figure out how to care for these children; and get on with my life as God's prophet to these errant people.*" Right? Wrong. The rigor of obedience was still to hold sway.

> "*The Lord said to me, 'Go, show your love to your wife again, though she is loved by another man and is an adulteress. Love her as the Lord loves the Israelites, though they turn to other gods and love the sacred raisin cakes.' So I bought her for fifteen shekels of silver and about a homer and a lethek of barley. Then I said to her, 'You are to live with me many days; you must not be a prostitute or be intimate with any man, and I will behave the same way toward you.'"*
>
> Hosea 3:1-3

We understand that Hosea's marriage is illustrative of the prophetic message God called him to proclaim to Israel. As Hosea was married literally to an unfaithful wife, God was married symbolically to an unfaithful people with whom

He had established a covenant relationship. The prophet's union with a woman who preferred to sleep around mirrored Israel's apostasy and worship of other gods. And as Hosea would eventually offer his unfaithful wife forgiveness and reconciliation, God too would continue to offer forgiveness to His wayward people.

Notwithstanding these overarching themes of the book of Hosea, there flows through them, the rigor the prophet knew in his personal life with Gomer and in his public life of "Hear the word of the Lord, you Israelites." His responsibility to balance the two callings—maintaining a union with an unfaithful wife as an illustration of God's union with an unfaithful people, and proclaiming that to an unrepentant nation—was without doubt onerous and burdensome. That, we can take to the bank.

Finale

From the Books of Genesis to Malachi, the Old Testament traces via the lives of our biblical ancestors the relationship God sought to have with His people. Through the lens of the Bible and biblical scholarship in the preceding chapters, we have walked with just a few of them on their journeys. Their decisions to respond in faith, obedience, and courage to God's call speak through the millennia to us. As their stories give testament, the rigor in God's call to follow Him is difficult, demanding, strenuous, tough, hard, ill-timed, exasperating, contrary, trying, dangerous, and often belies common sense. Yet they hiked up their robes and did just that.

In faith, with obedience and courage, we are called to the same.

Part II

God's Call to Jesus

*"Then God said, 'Let **us** make mankind in **our** image, in **our** likeness..."*
Genesis 1:26, emphasis mine

This divine declaration was not understood in ancient times to reference the *royal we* pronoun form usage of kings and queens in monarchies not yet formed. But there is purpose in every word God speaks. I believe the purpose in this verse is to authenticate that God's Son, who came to be called Jesus, was connate in God's plans from the beginning. In other words, the pronouns *us* and *our* reference Jesus and God, in whose image mankind was to be made. Both Father and Son were witnesses to the eons of human evolution. God's Son watched as Adam and Eve fell prey to Satan's wiles in the garden; sorrowed over mankind's first murder and its consequences; and over the millenniums, agonized as the seesaw of unfaithfulness of the people They created tethered up and down in human history.

Yes, there were periods when the created seemed to be in one accord with the Creator. But obedience and faithfulness never stuck. No Gorilla Glue stick could bind the people to their God for very long. And so, it came to pass, some 4,000 plus years later, that God the Father called His Son to enter the fray. (Author's Note: Contentious debate seeking to reconcile a creation timeline continues to this day. It is not my intent to add fodder to these arguments.) For Jesus it was not an unexpected call. He knew it was inherent in God's original plan. Privy to it from the beginning, He simply waited as human history continued to unfold, and God's call to Him finally came.

A long-standing tenet of the Jewish faith was that a Messiah was to come. In the first book of the Bible, the patriarch Jacob proclaimed,

"The scepter will not depart from Judah, nor the ruler's staff from between his feet, until he to whom it belongs shall come and the obedience of the nations shall be his."

Genesis 49:10

The *he* so referenced was that Messiah. Among the major prophets, Isaiah's prophesies about the first coming of Jesus were quoted often.

"Therefore, the Lord himself will give you a sign: The virgin will conceive and give birth to a son, and will call him Immanuel."

Isaiah 7:14

"For a child is born, to us a son is given, and the government

will be on his shoulders. And he will be called Wonderful Counselor, Mighty God, Everlasting Father, Prince of Peace."
Isaiah 9:6

"A shoot will come up from the stump of Jesse, from his roots a Branch will bear fruit. The Spirit of the Lord will rest upon him…"
Isaiah 11:1

Both the 53rd and 61st chapters of Isaiah offer further prophesies of Jesus' coming; the latter of which Jesus himself would read to his hometown and proclaim thereafter,

"Today this scripture is fulfilled in your hearing."
Luke 4:21

Understood in the prophesies of Jeremiah and Micah are references to the promise of God to send a king who would bring peace to His people and the world.

"The day is coming, God said, "when I will make a new covenant with the people of Israel and Judah."
Jeremiah 31:31

"But you Bethlehem Ephrathah, though you are small among the clans of Judah, out of you will come for me one who will be ruler over Israel, whose origins are from of old, from ancient times."
Micah 5:2

Three familiar prophesies of the prophet Zechariah point

clearly to Jesus as the coming Messiah—He would ride into Jerusalem on a donkey (Zechariah 9:9); He would be betrayed with 30 pieces of silver (Zechariah 11:130); When He is struck down, i.e. crucified, His sheep will scatter (Zechariah 13:7). The Apostle Matthew quotes the prophet Hosea, *"And so was fulfilled what the Lord had said through the prophet, 'Out of Egypt I called my son.'"* (Matthew 2:15)

God would eventually send His "one and only son" to be the Savior of humanity. And though that sending was divinely ordained, it would not be without rigor for the One sent.

Jesus' Rigor

"In your relationships with one another, have the same mindset as Christ Jesus: Who, being in very nature God, did not consider equality with God something to be used to his own advantage; rather, he made himself nothing by taking the very nature of a servant, being made in human likeness. And being found in appearance as a man, he humbled himself by becoming obedient to death—even death on a cross."
Philippians 2:5-8

The Apostle Paul penned these words in an epistle to the church at Philippi. The scripture provides insight into Christ Jesus' character and nature. Though one with God, He willingly surrendered His divinity and equality in obedience to God's call. The rigor for our Savior began before His birth in a manger. At the moment He submitted to His Father's will, He subjected himself to the difficulties faced by all who answered the Lord's call. That preordained decision to deny His divinity became the change agent of mankind's salvation. To accomplish this meant Christ's shunning of the splendors of heaven to embrace the squalor of earth. The reality of incarnation would test His resolve; and like His human ancestors, He would know the rigor of obedience.

As an infant Jesus would not have known the conditions of His birth to an unattended teenage mother in a shelter for animals. But we know enough of history to understand that those conditions were not favorable for either of them. Added to the physical difficulties they faced was the death threat for all Jewish boys ages two and under issued by King Herod. (Matthew 2: 13-16) As directed by God, Joseph and Mary fled with baby Jesus to Egypt where they stayed as aliens until Herod's death.

If their experiences in a foreign land were anything akin to those of today's refugees who seek asylum in this country, we can imagine the hardships faced by the young child and his parents. The scriptures do little to satisfy our thirst for the details of Jesus' childhood. We imagine that as the son of a carpenter, he learned the trade of carpentry; but even that is supposition as no scripture speaks to it directly.

Our clearest sense of the kind of boy he was is offered in the story of his brief separation from his parents during an annual trip to Jerusalem to celebrate the Festival of the Passover. On the second day of travel back home, Mary and Joseph realized Jesus was not with others of their party. Returning with anxiety to Jerusalem, they searched three days. Finally, on that third day they found Him in the temple, holding court with the teachers. Exasperated (and probably more than just exasperated, but this is the Bible and the typical expressions a parent in that circumstance might have uttered are thus prohibited), His mother says, "*Son, why have you treated us like this? Your father and I have been anxiously searching for you."* Jesus replies, *"Why were you searching for me? Didn't you know I had to be in my Father's house?"* Or as recorded in the King James Version, *"I must be about my Father's business?* (Luke 2:48-49)

Though the scriptures reveal that His parents were baffled by His answer, Jesus' response confirms that at age 12, He fully understood His calling. And understanding that call meant He knew He was more than a biological son; He was the Son of God. The scriptures proclaim that upon the return to Nazareth, Jesus was thereafter obedient to his parents, and that He *"grew in wisdom and stature, and in favor with God and man."* (Luke 2:51-52) We are left to wonder if that description of the kind of young man he grew to be would have bearing upon His three-year ministry of soul salvation.

Not until age 33 did Jesus begin to be about His father's business; to jumpstart the accomplishment of the task to which God called Him. We don't know why it took that long to begin His ministry. We do know that during that historical period, the years between late teens and 20s were ones during which most young people would have been betrothed, married, and starting a family. Responding to God's call required Jesus to forego those cultural norms.

That decision in His human state would be a difficult one; in those moments of His humanness, He would know the rigor of the call. Obedience to God demanded He disavow the traditions of family life and choose instead the trying life of an itinerant preacher. The Gospels of Matthew, Mark and Luke give strikingly similar accounts of the beginning of that life.

> *"Then Jesus came from Galilee to the Jordan to be baptized by John.... As soon as Jesus was baptized, he went out of the water. At that moment heaven was opened, and he saw the Spirit of God descending like a dove and alighting on him. And a voice from heaven said, 'This is my Son, whom I love; with him I am well pleased.'"*
> Matthew 3:13-17; Mark 1:9-11; Luke 3:21-23

Almost immediately following His baptism, Jesus faced the first of the multiple rigors that would stalk His ministry during the next three years. Over a 40-day period, the devil tested Jesus' obedience to God. Despite His hunger and weakness, Jesus met each temptation with the word of His Father. Following that battle of the spirit, Jesus returned to Nazareth and standing in the synagogue, read from the scroll of Isaiah, *"The Spirit of the Lord is on me, because he has anointed me to proclaim good news to the poor. He has sent me to proclaim freedom for the prisoners and recovery of sight for the blind, to set the oppressed free, to proclaim the year of the Lord's favor....* He then said to those gathered, *"Today this scripture is fulfilled in your hearing."* (Luke 4:16-21)

One might think such an announcement by a hometown boy grown into manhood would be met with enthusiasm; one of their own the long-awaited messiah! Following the ordeal in the wilderness, rejection by those whom He knew and probably counted as friends, if not extended family, had to have been devastating. He would have wanted salvation for them first and foremost. But as scripture records, the people were furious at Jesus' words and audacity. His hometown attempted to throw Him off a cliff; they would rather see Him dead than accept His message. Though His divine nature knew this would be the outcome, His human nature must still have felt the weariness of the mission before Him.

Jesus knew His incarnation would require balancing His divinity with His humanity. From the divine perspective, He didn't need anyone to help with the work set before Him. But to rely upon His divinity alone would defeat the purpose for which He had come. His mission was to restore the relationship between mankind and God; to accomplish that He needed to empower others to carry on the work after His ultimate sacrifice.

Enter stage left: the ordinary men who would come to be known as Jesus' disciples. As the Bible depicts each encounter that resulted in them leaving their families and livelihood to follow Jesus, we are left to wonder, why them? During the ensuing three years, as demonstrated by their actions, they would weary the Savior; try His patience; and who knows, perhaps make Him wonder Himself why He chose them. But His three-year ministry with them would prove to be the bedrock upon which the Jesus movement grew and flourished.

The rigor of Jesus' call to obedience never faltered; as the three years counted down, it grew more odious. Physical threats were common. His message was ridiculed and rejected by the priests and leaders of the Jewish community. Even those closest to Him sometimes doubted and disappointed Him; and in the end, betrayed Him. Without doubt though, the most harrowing of Jesus' call to obedience was His acceptance of the cross. Jesus came knowing that in coming, in that brief time as one of the created, the end would be His crucifixion—the ultimate rigor.

As did those who were called before Him, Jesus did not

turn away from God's call or that rigor. *"My Father, if it is not possible for this cup to be taken away unless I drink it, may your will be done."*

Part III

Jesus' Call to the Disciples

If there is truth to the adage, "The apple doesn't fall too far from the tree," we see it unfold when Jesus began to *"be about His Father's business."* As His Father had before Him when He called the prophets of old to follow His dictates to be, to do, and to go, Jesus called 12 contemporaries to follow Him as He moved about the regions preaching, *"Repent, for the kingdom of heaven has come near."* (Matthew 4:17)

The Gospels offer varying accounts of how most of those who came to be known as Jesus' Disciples were selected. Jesus' call to them was simple: *"Follow me."* Seeing the brothers Simon, called Peter, and Andrew, Jesus spoke, *"Come, follow me and I will send you out to fish for people"* (Matthew 4:19); continuing from that place, Jesus came upon the brothers James and John in a boat preparing their fishing nets with their father, Zebedee. He called them and they left their boat and their father to follow Jesus. At another time Jesus saw a Jewish tax collector named Levi/Matthew at his tax collector's booth, and without preamble said, *"Follow me,"* and Matthew left his business to do just that. (Matthew 9:9)

The Gospel of John records Jesus issuing the same command, "*Follow me,*" to Philip; and he in turn found Nathaniel who proclaimed, "*Rabbi, you are the Son of God; you are the king of Israel.*" (John 1:44-49)

We have no timeframe for how long it took Jesus to assemble this team, but eventually, He appointed the 12.

> *"Simon(to whom he gave the name Peter), James son of Zebedee and his brother John (to whom he gave the name Boanerges, which means "sons of thunder"), Andrew, Philip, Bartholomew/Nathaniel, Matthew, Thomas, James son of Alphaeus, Thaddaeus, Simon the Zealot, and Judas Iscariot, who betrayed him."*
>
> Mark 3:16-19

These were ordinary men called to extraordinary rigor in following Jesus and His "Great Commission."

9

THE DISCIPLES' RIGOR

At the onset, answering affirmatively to Jesus' call to discipleship might not have been that difficult. The actions of The Twelve suggest as much. He called; they followed. These ordinary Galilean men knew enough of Jewish tradition to believe God's promise to one day send a king to deliver and restore Israel to its former position of power and independence. If this man Jesus was that person, then becoming part of His *executive council* would have its merits. After all, there was something about this stranger from Nazareth that was different. He spoke with authority; He was quietly charismatic; His pull was magnetic. If He was the promised Messiah, then what answer to His call could there be except, "Yes." Who wouldn't want to be counted among the restorers of the nation?

Jesus' charge to the 12 disciples as recorded in the Gospels of Mark and Luke is almost identical. Only the notation in Mark that Jesus sent them out two by two is missing in Luke's account.

"When Jesus had called the Twelve together, he gave them

power and authority to drive out all demons and to cure diseases, and he sent them out to proclaim the kingdom of God and to heal the sick. He told them: 'Take nothing for the journey – no staff, no bag, no bread, no money, no extra shirt.' ... So, they set out and went from village to village, proclaiming the good news and healing people everywhere."
Luke 9:6

With these instructions, the disciples knew their service in Jesus' *army* was not to be what they might have imagined. Here was no king on a mighty stallion leading them on their donkeys into battle against the Roman oppressors. There would be no military campaign to restore Israel; no guerilla warfare conducted in the streets and alleyways of Jerusalem to wear down the enemy's forces. Quite the opposite. As Mark records, in pairs, they were to engage in spreading the good news of the long-awaited Messiah on foot, with not even their staff for support as they walked; shouldering no backpack with provisions or a change of clothes; and no financial resources to sustain themselves. This was what following Jesus would constitute; this would be the rigor of their obedience to His call.

During Jesus' three years of direct ministry, the disciples gradually grew in their faith. As with any inchoate newbie, they crawled before they could stand. After standing, they walked haltingly, stumbling and sometimes falling. Often Jesus expressed His frustration at their ambivalence, doubt and weakness.

"You of little faith, he said, why did you doubt?"
Matthew 17:31

"Truly I tell you," Jesus answered, "this very night before the roster crows three times you will disown me."
Matthew 26:34

"Then the disciples came to Jesus in private and asked, 'Why couldn't we drive it [a demon] out?' He replied, 'Because you have so little faith...'"
Matthew 17:19-20

With hindsight we see those bumbling faith experiences as part of Jesus' fast-track, hands-on lesson plan for the men He would trust to spread the Gospel when He was no longer in their midst. After He ascended into heaven and they received the Holy Spirit at Pentecost, The Twelve would spread out from Jerusalem as Jesus directed;

"Therefore go and make disciples of all nations, baptizing them in the name of the Father and of the Son and of the Holy Spirit, and teaching them to obey everything I have commanded you. And surely I am with you always until the very end of the age."
Matthew 28:19-20

As they obeyed this commission, each would know rigor far surpassing the inconveniences they suffered while Jesus had walked alongside them.

In a secular culture that thrived in direct opposition to all Jesus taught, The Twelve faced ridicule, threats, and persecution as they strived to persuade both Jews and Gentiles to accept Jesus' message. We have no definitive information regarding the specifics of their ministries, nor how long each of them lived; and beyond Judas and James, and perhaps Peter, only tradition as to when and where they died. We know that they labored throughout the Roman Empire; and as suggested by biblical scholarship, in areas of the Middle East, Africa, and India.

In those travels, they experienced rigor in multiple dimensions. Easily seen in excavated ruins of biblical times are the roads of uneven stones and rocks upon which they trod. No rest stops dotted the landscape along the way. And as they moved farther from Jerusalem, strangers in foreign lands, preaching an even stranger message, they faced the opposition of pagan practices and beliefs. Their decision to obey Jesus' summons, *"follow me,"* translated into a life of suffering, and ended in most cases in a violent death.

- Peter—crucified upside down at his request in Rome during the persecution under Emperor Nero
- Andrew—said to have been crucified
- Thomas—thought to have died by sword piercing in and around India
- Philip—Put to death by a Roman proconsul for converting his wife to Christianity
- Matthew—some reports that he was stabbed to death in Ethiopia; others that he was not martyred
- Bartholomew/Nathaniel—accounts vary as to how he was martyred
- James, son of Zebedee—recorded in the Bible as having been put to death by the sword as ordered by King Herod
- James, son of Alphaeus—reported by the Jewish historian Josephus to have been stoned and then clubbed to death

- Simon the Zealot—killed supposedly after refusing to sacrifice to the sun god in Persia
- Matthias (Judas' replacement)—tradition suggests he was put to death by burning
- John—the only disciple thought to have escaped a violent death and dying from natural causes in his old age

For a moment, reflect upon what these original disciples faced both during Jesus' time with them and afterwards when He was not. They gave up livelihoods, turned from family, endured the struggles of an itinerant lifestyle, and watched in despair as the one for whom they had done all this died on a cross. After He disappeared from their sights, they would not return to the life they knew before they knew Him. No, they would part ways, each going to some far off, unknown region to do what Jesus had called them to do. In the strength and power of the Holy Spirit, they faced the rigor of that calling with courage, trust and faith.

Part IV

JESUS' CALL TO THE APOSTLE PAUL

Beyond the 12 Jesus initially called to discipleship was one destined to hear Jesus' call several years following His death and resurrection. At first glance Saul seems the least likely person Jesus would select. Ironically, at the time he heard the divine voice of Jesus, he was on a mission as one of the religious establishment's *hit men*, to round up Jesus' followers and bring them to the Jewish authorities.

Jesus' call to Paul, using his Jewish name Saul, was dramatically different than the simple, "*Follow me,*" to the OD's (original disciples). Perhaps it was because they were simple men that getting their attention required only a simple command. Paul was different. He was a Jewish Roman citizen and the son of a Pharisee. Growing up in the city of Tarsus, one of the largest trading centers of that time, he was no country bumpkin. An educated, urbane man, his epistles were written in the Greek language confirming his educational background. In his own words he stated, "*I studied under Gamliel and was thoroughly trained in the law of our ancestors.*"

As a strict adherent to Jewish law, this new religion would

have been an affront to all he held dear. In contemporary speak, we would pronounce Paul a definite enemy of the people who followed Christ. Yet, Jesus called him. He was to become the chosen instrument of God to proclaim the Lord's name to the Gentiles. (Acts 9:15-16)

As did the original Twelve, all of whom except John were martyred, Paul would know the rigor of obedience to God's call. Like his predecessors, in faith and with courage he would respond. And as both biblical and secular history proceeded to record, only Jesus himself would have a more profound impact upon the spread of Christianity than he did.

10

Apostle Paul's Rigor

The manner in which the Apostle Paul was summoned to the rigor of Jesus' call was so much more dramatic than that of The Twelve. At the time of their call, each had been engaged in rather mundane pursuits when the Savior strolled by and said, "Follow me." With little fanfare, they had done so. But the call to the Jewish fanatic intolerant of religious beliefs beyond his own was more reminiscent of how God had spoken to the prophets of old—directly and in the case of Moses, face to face.

Someone once wrote, "Sometimes a man meets his destiny on the road he took to avoid it." We see this in Paul's story.

At all costs, he wanted to be among those who stopped the spread of the Jesus movement. No doubt he envisioned that as his destiny. But traveling on that Damascus Road with intent to persecute the Lord's disciples, he would meet destiny head on when a light from heaven stopped him and he fell to the ground. Blinded in that moment of Jesus' power, a voice spoke, "*Saul, Saul, why do you persecute me?*" In answer to Saul's question, *"Who are you, Lord?"* the voice responded,

"I am Jesus, whom you are persecuting. Now get up and go into the city, and you will be told what you must do."

The first thing Paul had to do was locate a man named Ananias, a Jesus follower no less, to whom the Lord had given instructions relative to this infamous enemy of The Way (the name by which Jesus' disciples were first identified). The irony of his situation was priceless. Those against whom he had uttered "murderous threats" were the same people to whom he had been sent to regain his physical sight and spiritual insight necessary for what would become his life's work. What better way to confront Jews wrapped in the tentacles of Jewish laws and traditions that kept them from believing in Jesus, and Gentiles with their pagan beliefs and practices than to send a heretofore vehement proclaimer of that law. As the Lord said to Ananias when he hesitated in helping Saul/Paul,

> *"This man is my chosen instrument to proclaim my name to the Gentiles and their kings and to the people of Israel. I will show him how much he will suffer for my name."*
> Acts 9:15-16

That suffering began almost immediately after he regained his sight and in his converted identity sought fellowship with the very Jesus followers he was known to persecute. Understandably so, his proclamations in the synagogue that Jesus was the Son of God fell upon incredulous and suspicious ears. In time a conspiracy formed to kill this persecutor of the faith turned proclaimer of the same; only the timely action of a few who believed him prevented the tragedy.

According to biblical history, following his conversion

experience and nascent efforts to preach, Paul disappeared from ancient records for 12 years or so. The assumption is that he spent those years somewhere in the Arabian desert; a preparatory period perhaps of reconciling his Jewish theology with the gospel of Jesus. Following this "conversion sealing time" (my term), Paul commenced the missionary travels that sparked the spread of Christianity throughout the Middle East, Europe, and Africa. The rigor of his calling would mark those journeys as Jesus' words marked his life. He would indeed suffer for the name of the One who called him.

The Book of Acts chronicles the three missionary journeys of Paul, the initial one prompted by the Holy Spirit,

> *"While they were worshipping the Lord and fasting, the Holy Spirit said, 'set apart for me Barnabas and Saul for the work to which I have called them.'"*
>
> Acts 13:2

Thus they were sent by church leaders to take the gospel westward. Biblical accounts vary regarding the length of time of these missionary trips, but general consensus is that Paul spent 10 to 12 years traveling by ship and land before his final trip to Jerusalem.

On that first journey, he sailed across the Mediterranean Sea to Cyprus and other regions of the area. As they proclaimed the good news of Jesus, they drew the ire of Jewish leaders who resented the large crowds that gathered to hear him. A plot to both stone and kill them sent the men fleeing to Lystra and Derbe. Jewish opposition continued though, and before long, Paul came under fire again. He was dragged from the city, stoned and left for dead. These physical attacks,

however, did not deter him from God's call to spread the word. As he endured pain and deprivation, the rigor of his calling mounted. As Jesus had declared, he suffered.
- In the Roman colony of Philippi, he and Silas were severely flogged and thrown into jail. (Acts 16:19-24)
- In Jerusalem, he was beaten by a Jewish mob, arrested by the Roman soldiers and held in chains in their barracks.
- A Jewish conspiracy grew to kill the apostle.
- King Agrippa sent him as a prisoner to Rome and on the way there, shipwrecked by a violent storm, he was forced to swim to the shore of the island of Malta.
- As he awaited rescue with surviving shipmates, he was bitten by a snake.

In his own words, Paul described the rigor borne in God's call:

> *"We do not want you to be uninformed, brothers and sisters, about the troubles we experienced in the province of Asia. We were under great pressure far beyond our ability to endure, so that we despaired of life itself. Indeed, we felt we had received the sentence of death."*
> 2 Corinthians 1:8-9

> *"That is why, for Christ's sake, I delight in weaknesses, in insults, in hardships, in persecutions, in difficulties…"*
> 2 Corinthians 12:10

In the known records of the founders of our faith following Jesus' ascension, few of his time are recognized to have had the impact upon the spread of Christianity as did the

Apostle Paul. He is credited with the establishment of at least twenty churches from Syria to Italy during his 20-plus years of missionary work within the Roman Empire. His epistles account for 13 of the 27 books in the New Testament. Those writings alone have shaped Christianity as we know it today.

Yet none of these achievements came without cost. The price was paid in the rigor embedded in Paul's obedience to God's calling. As had the 12 disciples who knew Jesus before him, Paul followed the Savior with the same courage, trust and faith as they did. Neither they nor he were immune to suffering as a result; they understood and accepted it as the hallmark of the rigor of God's call.

Finale

God's call to His Son and Jesus' subsequent call to the twelve disciples and the apostle Saul/Paul illuminates the rigor inherent therein. The foundation of Christianity rests upon a bedrock of rigor. If no rigor abides in the faith confession, the question looms, "Is it a faith confession?"

The accounts of the faith responses of the disciples and the apostle as demonstrated by their actions speak to what an affirmative answer to Jesus means. Duplicity cannot exist in that affirmation. The challenges that face those who hear God's call must be met with courage, trust and faithfulness. The rigor of the call demands and allows nothing less.

During the Apostolic Age, these men—the twelve disciples and Paul—would turn the world upside down as the Jesus movement would not be stopped; and Christianity became a dominant religious faith.

Part V

God's Call to 21st Century Christians

"*Where are you?*"

God's primeval question to our biblical ancestors as recorded in Genesis 3:9 is still His call to us today. They, seeking to avoid responding to Him, hid among the trees and foliage of Eden. We mimic that antediluvian behavior by hiding in our modern-day gardens of acquisition, self-aggrandizement, pursuit of fame and fortune, prestige, and power. We seek escape from His scrutiny and as importantly His call.

Why? Because like Adam and Eve, we are disobedient. Though we claim Him as our God, His Son Jesus as our Savior, and Christianity as our faith, our actions belie our beliefs.

Why have we lost the distinguishing marks of our faith as Christians? Why are we hiding from Christ in our modern gardens? Perhaps the answer lies in the conundrum of Christianity itself. For the 21st century Christian, being "like Christ" is as challenging as trying to get the wrong jigsaw piece to fit in the puzzle. More than challenging, it seems impossible. These millennia later, God's call is as it was for our ancestors, easy to affirm, difficult to execute; and in that conflict rests the rigor.

11

THE RIGOR OF 21ST CENTURY CHRISTIAN IDENTITY

As mentioned in the Introduction, more than two billion people identify themselves as Christians. Whether Catholic or Protestant, they came to that identification primarily through denominational rituals or traditions. For many, infant baptism and confirmation rituals under the auspices of a church stamped them Christians. Others laid claim through their public acceptance of Christ at that time in a worship service when the invitation to discipleship and church membership sounded from the pulpit. Reception into church membership sealed their identity as Christians. Still others simply heard the gospel message via some media and in that moment accepted Jesus in their hearts and called themselves Christians.

Irrespective of the mechanisms of the faith declaration, identifying as Christians (except in those areas of the world where the Christian faith remains under attack) was relatively benign for most. It takes little effort to recite the words of the Christian faith and lay claim to the moniker. But all too soon, many Christians face the reality that it is difficult to live in that identity. In truth, their identity as a Christian is typically overshadowed by their competing identities of job status, academic degrees, fraternal or social allegiances; any of the ways by which they are known. If identity is the characteristic that determines who a person is, why is Christian identity so challenging?

Perhaps Oswald Chambers helps us answer that question. He wrote, "What Jesus says is hard, it is only easy when it is heard by those who have his disposition."

That statement succinctly describes the difficulty, the challenge of Christian identity. Jesus' disposition is so unlike ours that it is a daily struggle to subjugate ours, to align it in some degree to that of the One with whom we identify. It's easy to understand why the famous Hindu lawyer and political ethicist Mahatma Gandhi was quoted as saying, if he could meet Christians who were like Christ, he'd become one too. A stinging commentary perhaps, but one that rightly speaks to the rigor of Christian identity.

The synoptic gospels reveal the nature of Jesus' disposition, His tendency to behave in ways that defined His character. From those scriptures recorded in Matthew, Mark, and Luke, we know from His actions that He is loving and kind; merciful and forgiving; humble and understanding; sympathetic and caring; a servant leader driven by a purpose to fulfill God's will. With no consideration of status or lack thereof, He healed a man with leprosy, a centurion's servant, a disciple's mother-in-law; two demon-possessed men; a paralyzed man. (Matthew 8-9).

In contrast, how hard it is for us to offer aid or assistance to the least and lost outside our spheres of family and friends. We are busy, struggling with personal challenges; the needs of others pale before our own. Though we are Christians, we cry out, "It's too much. It's too hard." We read of Jesus' concern for children, their value and the consequences of treating them in any manner that might damage their well-being and faith development. (Matthew 18-19) We mouth those sentiments even as we listen to or read reports of child abuse and neglect, of children underserved in schools and without adequate health care. Though we are Christians and lament their plight, we throw up our hands and ask, "What can we do? These issues are difficult and beyond our control."

The disparities between our dispositions and that of Jesus are too many to list. The point is clear. Identity as a Christian in a world that is the antithesis of Christ will require more than just the ritualistic profession of faith. If we are to be like Christ—the reason we became Christians—we must also address the rigor of that decision, understanding that identity is more than just name.

> *"Jesus said to his disciples, 'If any want to become my followers, let them deny themselves and take up their cross and follow me.'"*
> Matthew 6:24

True followers of Christ should expect ridicule, rejection and sometimes persecution because of that identity. In fact, identity as a Christian in the modern age is no different than identity was for a believer in God in ancient times. Recall the man Daniel whose identity as a God follower met resistance throughout his life. Despite captivity, servitude, and a lion's den he never hid his faith but confronted the difficulties of that God identity with courage, trust, and faith.

His actions that aligned with his faith convictions set him apart.

"The king said to Daniel, 'May your God whom you serve continually rescue you.'"
Daniel 6:15

Even the king who sentenced him to death knew he was a God follower; and that no hardship could alter his faith.

We are called to the same standard in our discipleship. Once we have professed Jesus as Lord of our lives, we are challenged to be who we say we are—Christians following in the footsteps of Christ. Set apart from the secular world by our confession of faith, we are called to wear the badge of that identity no matter the difficulties and the rigor faced in doing so with similar courage, trust and faith.

12

THE RIGOR OF 21ST CENTURY CHRISTIAN OBEDIENCE

Most certainly conjoined, Christian Identity and Obedience stand as sentinels of Christianity. Once Identity is professed, Obedience follows. Right? If the contemporary human condition is an indicator of the supposition, then the answer is No. Unfortunately, to my knowledge there exists no obedience measurement system that points to how many of the 2.2 billion professed Christians are obedient to Christ. When asked by an expert in the law what was the greatest commandment, Jesus replied,

> *"Love the Lord your God with all your heart and with all your soul and with all your mind. This is the first and greatest commandment. And the second is like it. Love your neighbor as yourself."*
>
> Matthew 22:35-39

Those two commandments and His Great Commission,

> *"Therefore go and make disciples of all nations, baptizing*

them in the name of the Father and of the Son and of the Holy Spirit, and teaching them to obey everything I have commanded you."
Matthew 28:19-20

are binding still. They are the operative words for understanding Christian obedience. Those who seek to be His disciples must embrace them.

Yet, as it is with our identity as Christians, our obedience to Christ is not easy. In error we believe that the simple confession of faith will shield us from life's difficulties and not require of us anything too taxing. But that is not what the Christian faith implies. Rather, as Oswald Chambers writes in My Utmost for His Highest, "If we are going to be disciples of Jesus, we have to remember that all noble things are difficult. The Christian life is gloriously difficult…" And as recorded throughout the New Testament, obedience to Christ's calling is hard; its rigor never-ending for all who choose to follow Him.

Perhaps the most difficult aspect of Christian obedience is found in our attempt to strike a balance between what Christ commanded and what the contemporary age dictates as the norm. We live in an era of self-indulgence, excessive consumption, relaxed mores, idolatry of technology, lust for fame and fortune, and the unending biases and prejudices that have marked humanity from its inception. Bombarded with what we perceive as our reality, we strive to shape our Christian faith to fit within the confines of our secular strivings.

To be honest, it's so much easier to conform to the secular than the sacred. Yes, Jesus said,

"If you love those who love you, what credit is that?... if you do good to those who are good to you, what credit is that? And if you lend to those from whom you expect repayment, what credit is that to you?"
                                                            Luke 6-27-35

But the times are different, we rationalize. *We can't just give what we've worked for to whoever asks. Isn't that why local municipalities and non-profit organizations operate shelters and offer services to help the less fortunate?*

Jesus' teachings fly in the face of the rationality of 21st century believers are forced to face. Christians sway dangerously attempting to walk the high wire between His commands and secular realities. Avoiding a fall is not easy.

As proof, consider the overwhelming, seemingly ubiquitous impact of social and electronic media upon contemporary life—televisions in practically every conceivable space, cell phones in every hand from highchair to wheelchair capturing *selfies* and other self-indulgences, virtual games and avatars that mimic or reimagine life. Juxtapose these living frames of our lives with the great commandments of Jesus. Are they compatible? Not in the least.

Loving God as Jesus commanded is all but impossible in a culture that has elevated self-love to idolatry. Likewise, loving our neighbor as we love ourselves requires of us an absence of self-hatred, of prejudice and bias, of hubris and pride. Cultivating a spirit of generosity, of kindness, of not being judgmental, of turning the other cheek, of forgiving, of extending mercy in the face of injustice demands even more. For the professing Christian, these are among the rigors of obedience.

Though they are daunting and sometimes seem impossible, they come with the territory of being a disciple of Jesus. But they do not, as Oswald Chambers writes, "make us faint or cave in." Enduring and mastering the rigor of obedience to the call of Jesus is possible with courage, trust, and faith. He comes to us with pierced hands demanding that we remember Him who in obedience to God was not felled by the rigor required of that obedience. When we claim these attributes of Jesus as our own, we can be the Daniels of our day—and like him, live out our faith in total surrender to our God.

13

THE RIGOR OF 21ST CENTURY CHRISTIAN LABOR

> *"Then he said to his disciples, 'The harvest is plentiful but the workers are few. Ask the Lord of the harvest, therefore to send out workers into his harvest field.'"*
> Matthew 9:37-38

Critical to the bedrock of the Christian faith is its work, its deeds; of believers laboring in the vineyards of humanity bringing the same gospel Jesus and His followers brought 2,000-plus years ago. That labor required them to move in and about their world sowing the messages of the two Great Commandments: *Love the one and only God with all your heart, soul and mind, worshipping no other god but Him; and love your neighbor as you love yourself*, and the Great Commission, *Make disciples of all nations, baptize them and teach them to obey My commandments.*

We know from both scripture and biblical history the difficulties and hardships those early Christians faced as they toiled to do as Jesus commanded. We can confirm the fruit of that labor these 20 centuries later. With a professed 2.2 billion Christians on the planet, one might be persuaded the labor is completed. But that assumption would be false. Despite the numbers, the reality is that the labor Jesus called His believers to do then remains now. It remains primarily because the professions of faith have proved shallow. In this modern age, as in ancient times, believers deny Jesus and deny God by their actions.

Confronted with the rigor of the work required of their profession, too often what we see is what we get. And what we get in the 21st century is Christians confronting the practicalities of living the Great Commandments and the Great Commission with little will or resolve to be obedient to them. Such a pronouncement might on surface seem severe. But a close look at the heart of Christianity today sustains it.

With Jehovah's role relegated primarily to mentions in Saturday or Sunday church services; with the separation of church and state foundational in the ideology of the largest of Christian nations; with historical precedents that still continue to pervert Jesus' message for secular gains; Christians seeking to be true to their faith profession do so weighed by a twisted faith. There is absolute rigor in that effort for believers struggling to keep faith ships afloat in the sea of 21st century culture.

It's mighty hard to advocate loving only the God of our faith profession, and worshipping just Him in a culture that has raised high places for contemporary gods that rival His sovereignty. Such is the world in which we live that value and worth are gleaned, not from God nor from Jesus, but from the personalities of power opined by man. Even diligent believers struggle with subjugation of self to actually and intentionally live Christian principles. Perks and privileges appear just rewards.

Adoption of the Apostle Paul's attitude as recorded in his epistle to the believers in Philippi is most difficult:

> *"But whatever were gains to me I now consider loss for the sake of Christ. What is more, I consider everything a loss because of the surpassing worth of knowing Christ Jesus my Lord…"*
> Philippians 3:7-8

The difficulty rests in the all-encompassing attitude of our times that what we possess defines who we are, which in turn defines our worth. Such a belief system easily raises to god-like status practices that compromise our love of the God of our faith. Further, it moves us in the direction of *having other gods* before Him.

We have only to remember the man God chose to rule Israel after the death of King David—his son, Solomon. Subsequently blessed by God with wealth and wisdom beyond imagination, Solomon began his reign in obedience. He loved God and worshipped Him as the Law dictated. But in time, influenced by his desire to keep his enemies close—which he did by marrying their daughters—the pagan culture of those 1,000 wives and concubines of his harem had an unfortunate influence upon the king. His one and only God became just one of the many gods he worshipped.

Solomon's tragic fall from God's favor, brought about by his disobedience, is a reminder to 21st century Christians of the reality of what remains at stake today. We know that Solomon did not overnight adapt his religious beliefs to accommodate those of a pagan culture. The Bible records that as he grew older, he strayed from his faith. Like Solomon, we don't at first opportunity jump into bed with the contemporary lures of our time. As professed believers we strive to stay the course in our actions to love God and to have no other gods before us. But the enemy of our faith, as we know, is always on the prowl. When we lower our guard, he is there, offering for our consideration a course that belies the characteristics of our heavenly Father in seemingly small ways.

A vast majority of those two billion plus believers started their faith journey as children, growing up in homes that espoused Christian beliefs. The Bible was openly displayed; a children's Bible or storybook the norm for bedtime reading. Meals were preceded with a blessing of thanksgiving. Even in homes that lacked some of these amenities, faith in God and His teachings were essential elements of life. Sunday worship services, including Sunday school, set the tone for the upcoming week. These rituals and traditions helped shape spiritual identity. Over time as childhood gave away to adulthood, the principles of faith that were so ingrained and simple started to fray. The Word of God came under attack as the secular world squeezed its spirit; seeking to turn it toward apostasy.

Other professed believers who came to salvation well past childhood, often with little or no incentive to do so during those developmental years, joined the great migration to eternity and committed to the journey. They accepted Jesus as Savior and joined the church, bought a Bible, attended new member's classes, sang in the choir, offered their secular expertise to the labors of church committees. Private prayer and thanksgiving blessings grew to be routine. In time however, as with the aforementioned believers, the new identity began to lose its initial attraction and its sparkle faded. Secular practices and pursuits that had been forsaken for Christian principles reared dormant heads and slipped into loopholes of fraying, wavering faith.

It isn't necessarily that Christians want to avoid the labor inherent in their faith. It's more a sense that what they'd been pitched is not what they thought it would be. The message they heard and internalized was one of forgiven sin, reconciliation, grace, and love. They'd reasoned that the redeemed state bestowed by the mantle of Christianity would forestall difficulties common to the human experience; that surrendering their lives to Jesus would shelter them from the enemy's attacks.

To be honest, those assumptions are easy to understand. Talk of rigor in the context of faith is not known to enhance the message; just the opposite. Life is hard enough. If Christianity is difficult too, why sign up? It's a valid question.

21st century Christians engaged in both speaking and doing their faith are positioned to answer. They tell the truth; that God's sun shines and His rain falls upon both saint and sinner; the storms of illness, loss, disappointments, pain, and death inevitably come to all. Staying committed to God in the midst of such experiences is hard—but that is when the rubber meets the road. Understanding that salvation is not free; that it came with a price is crucial to understanding what it means to profess Christ. He paid the price for the forgiven sin and reconciliation we embrace, for the grace and love of God we eagerly accept. That cost however did not shield us from the downturns of humanity, but it did provide a track upon which we strive to walk in the midst of them.

Striving to stay on course on that track is hard. Sin controls the switch that alters the course we pursue. It derails the track, sending it in directions leading away from our profession of faith. We find ourselves laboring in vineyards not of Christianity, but of the secular. More often than not it is there, in the world of greed, pride, and lust, that we forget who we are, what we have professed, and the labor to which we have committed.

Scripture teaches that we will suffer trials for being Christians (1 Peter 4:12). The rigor of those fiery trials is germane to the faith. But alongside are the difficulties we self-impose when we give up on our profession because it's not the staircase to heaven we envisioned it to be.

Laboring in 21st century harvest fields is not easy. The siren songs of self-gratification, consumerism, peer pressure, narcissism, retail therapy, and non-medicinal opiates (those things that dull our senses to what it means to be a Christian) are a bear to resist. But if we are to claim the moniker, *Christian*, resist we must. God's clarion call requires our continued faith, trust and courage in spite of its rigor.

Part VI

FINAL THOUGHTS

The most difficult conundrum to face Christians since the inception of Christianity to the present age is the Apostle James' instruction to believers that we must be more than hearers of God's word. More importantly, we must be doers of it. (James 1:19-25) It is in the struggle to move from a profession of faith to the practice of that faith profession that most Christians run into the rigor of Jesus' call.

Few will deny that we 21st century Christians live in an era nowhere near one that would warm our Savior's heart. Rather, ours more fits the lyrics of the classic R&B song by the Temptations, "Ball of Confusion," which describes the mood of our contemporary world. Among the confusing aspects listed in that song are segregation, humiliation, aggravation, addiction, fear that we are living on the Eve of Destruction, bill collectors, evolution, revolution, gun control, tension, and the list goes on. Recorded in 1970, these lyrics describe a world in upheaval, uncertainty, and a host of other ills that eerily depict the world of today; a time when we glory in men rather than Jesus; a time when our sense of worth and value are gleaned not from Jesus nor from living His commandments, but from the personas of what rise to levels of success opined by man. The ancient trilogy of mankind's failures—greed, lust and pride—sway us from subjugation of self and living Christian principles as Jesus taught.

The lead story recently in Apple News detailed a shooting during a church service. A man stood and opened fire on the congregants, killing two of them. He was subsequently shot by security volunteers in the worship service who were armed. The law allows guns in places of worship in the state in which this tragedy occurred; and authorities, including the pastor were quick to applaud that law and the actions of the volunteers who are hailed as having prevented further mayhem.

When I read the account, I immediately thought of the incident in the Garden of Gethsemane when the Roman soldiers came to arrest Jesus. The impetuous Simon Peter immediately drew his sword and cut off the right ear of the high priest's servant in an apparent effort to protect Jesus. We know how the incident concluded. Jesus rebuked Peter's actions and miraculously healed the man's wound. His words found in Matthew 26:52-53 are iconic. *"'Put your sword back in its place,' Jesus said to him, 'for all who draw the sword will die by the sword.'"*

What would Jesus' response have been to the shooting incident described above? Are Christians in situations such as that one justified in taking the actions the security volunteers took? Is it appropriate for the spiritual head of the body of Christ to applaud their actions? What do Jesus' teachings say to his believers about violence and killing?

These are difficult questions—questions that confront believers with the rigor of their profession of faith; of their saying "Yes" to follow Jesus and to obey His commandments.

Psalm 60:3 reads, *"You have shown your people desperate times."* God continues to show His people times of desperation, of difficult and hard times; times like today when the world is a ball of confusion; times when the struggle to reconcile what we profess with what we practice is ever present. Accepting and acknowledging that the times are part and parcel of the Christian experience and the rigor wrought by them is meant as someone has said, "to make us, not break us," helps believers move closer to the image of Christ.

If that is indeed the goal of our faith, the question is simple: how do we get there? How do we become both professed and practicing Christians in this time, in this space? How does the image of Christ become our own?

We most certainly will not become what I term PPCs: "Professed AND Practicing Christians" by conforming to the culture of comfort that pervades the world in which we live. Nor will we by throwing in the towel; by giving up on the Christian life because the struggles seem unending despite what we do to be the people we think God wants us to be. Perhaps a sentiment attributed to Elbert Hubbard that is paraphrased in *Streams in the Desert* best expresses what PPCs must embrace in addressing the rigor of the Christian calling: *"God will examine your life not for medals, diplomas or degrees, but for battle scars."*

Those battle scars symbolize the rigor of responding in practice to the profession of faith. Like an anvil that strikes hard against metal to fashion it into the instrument or tool or treasure desired by the owner, so the rigor of God's call forms the character and disposition desired of God of those who profess His name.

To help us avoid both the traps of comfort and concession and choose authenticity over imitation, God gives us the third entity of the Holy Trinity—the Holy Spirit. It is in our embrace of the Holy Spirit, allowing it to give us guidance and correction, coupled with God's how-to manual, the Holy Scriptures, that teaches and gives light to the path we follow to become Christ-like.

There is no doubt it is hard to manage the rigor of our faith because there is a constant battle between our human, sinful nature and the spirit of God. Embodying the fruit of His spirit taxes us at every turn. We know how difficult it is to Love others, especially when we haven't learned to love ourselves. We misunderstand the meaning of joy, seeking it instead in the happenings of our lives and missing its true meaning. We seek peace in places least equipped to give it, missing its shoutouts in the words of the scripture. We ignore the concept of forbearance or tolerance to avoid the rigor in searching for truth. We eschew kindness except when it's extended to those who reciprocate. We qualify goodness to align with actions or behaviors that require little of us. Our faithfulness is contingent upon the other's extension of it. We reserve gentleness to our interactions with little children, unless they're getting on our last nerve! We practice self-control when said practice is easy; and lose it when things are not.

But we must remember that God provides us what we need to be strengthen rather than defeated by the rigor of His call. If we are willing; if we truly seek to follow Christ, the Holy Spirit awaits. With His promptings, His wisdom and direction, we can be among those who hear God's call, accept the rigor the response to it will bring, and press onward in faith to the prize in store for so doing. The greater the rigor we face, the closer we come to His image in our lives. Yes, *Hard things are hard.* But in and with Christ Jesus, all things are possible. Confronting the rigor imbedded in God's call is not an exception, but an expectation we embrace as we strive to bear His image.

ACKNOWLEDGEMENTS

Trust in the Lord with all your heart and lean not on your own understanding; in all your ways submit to him, and he will make your paths straight.
                                                            Proverbs 3:5-6

I give glory alone to God, my heavenly Father for His inspiration and prompting that led to the writing of this, my fourth book. If it has any worth or value, all credit goes to Him. I write in the Christian genre because it is where I best share the gift of word-craft God gave me. As I always say, as long as He so allows, I will write to glorify my Lord; and hopefully inspire others to know Him as I do. Within His word are treasures for a lifetime.

Once again, I must acknowledge that this manuscript, as with the one before it, would not have come to fruition without the critical ear of my BFF and sister in Christ, Ann Lloyd. She has listened to each section; offered from her perspective as student and teacher of the Bible insight and correction needed to refine the message. I am indebted to her and thankful for her insight and continuing encouragement. Team A&B always!

I remain always grateful to family members and friends near and far who continue to support my writing. They purchase my books and share them with others. And almost all of them await the next one.

Well, this is it—the next one. A different book in some ways. One that I trust will inspire reflection and self-accountability. As I hope you will acknowledge, saying *yes* is easy. It's putting that *yes* into practices that align with Jesus' teachings that is hard. Therein resides the rigor.

I am once again thankful to Word Crafts Press and Mike Parker, my publisher, for seeing merit in this effort and agreeing to publish this book.

Beverly ND Clopton

About the Author

The eldest of nine children, Beverly N.D. Clopton grew up in Dallas and completed her undergraduate studies in the great state of Texas before she embarked on a 40-year calling as a professional educator in the Dallas, Denver, and Los Angeles public school systems.

Stepping into retirement offered Beverly the opportunity to return to her first loves—the written word and the Word of God.

In addition to *Rigors of the Call*, she is the author of *Heaven or Bust: Journey to Glory, Sonshine: Reflections of Faith*, and her most recent book, *Surviving Pitfalls on the Path*.

Also Available From

WordCrafts Press

Trusting God Through Testing Times
  by Jill Grossman

I Am
  by Summer McKinney

Pondering(s) Too
  by Wayne Berry

Written That You May Believe
  by Rodney Boyd

I Wish Someone Had Told Met
  by Barbie Loflin

More Devotions from Everyday Things
  by Tammy Chandler

https://wordcrafts.net

www.ingramcontent.com/pod-product-compliance
Lightning Source LLC
Chambersburg PA
CBHW030158100526
44592CB00009B/339